THE GOLDEN AGE OF SMOKING

PUBLICATIONS: POETRY & PROSE
John Hartley Williams

A Dream Of Kos. Hans van Eijk at the Bonnefant Press 2013

Death Comes For The Poets (with Matthew Sweeney). Muswell Press, London 2012

Assault on the Clouds. Shoestring Press, Nottingham 2012

Hex Wheels. Hans van Eijk at the Bonnefant Press, 2011

Less of That W Or I'll Z You! Surrealist Editions, Leeds, 2011

A Poetry Inferno. Eyelet Press, Nottingham, 2011

Outpost Theatre. Hans van Eijk at the Bonnefant Press, 2009

Café des Artistes. Jonathan Cape, 2009

Pistol Sonnets. Salt Publishing, 2008

The Ship. Salt Publishing, 2007

Blues. Jonathan Cape, 2004.

Teach Yourself Poetry Writing (Third edition, with Matthew Sweeney). Hodder & Stoughton, 2008

North Sea Improvisation, a Fotopoem. Aark Arts, 2003.

Mystery in Spiderville. Jonathan Cape, 2002 (Revised edition: Vintage, 2003).

Spending Time with Walter. Jonathan Cape, 2001.

Censored Poems. Translations of Marin Sorescu. Bloodaxe Books, 2001.

Canada. Bloodaxe Books, 1997.

Teach Yourself Poetry Writing (with Matthew Sweeney). Hodder, 1996.

Ignoble Sentiments. Arc Press, July 1995.

Double. Bloodaxe Books, 1994.

Cornerless People. Bloodaxe Books, 1990.

Bright River Yonder. Bloodaxe Books, 1987.

Hidden Identities. Chatto & Windus, 1982.

THE GOLDEN AGE OF SMOKING

John Hartley Williams

Shoestring Press

Printed by imprintdigital
Upton Pyne, Exeter
www.imprintdigital.net

Typeset by narrator
www.narrator.me.uk
enquiries@narrator.me.uk

Published by Shoestring Press
19 Devonshire Avenue, Beeston, Nottingham, NG9 1BS
(0115) 925 1827
www.shoestringpress.co.uk

First published 2014
© Copyright: John Hartley Williams

The moral right of the author has been asserted.

ISBN 978 1 907356 98 8

ACKNOWLEDGEMENTS

Poems previously published in:

Agenda
Ambit
Angel Exhaust
Dark Horse
Dwang
Edinburgh Review
London Review of Books
Phosphor
PN Review
Poetry Review
Salzburg Poetry Review
Spectator
Staple
Tears in the Fence
The Same (USA)
Warwick Review

We flicked the flashlight
And there was the ferryman just as Virgil
And Dante had seen him. He looked at us coldly
And his eyes were dead and his hands on the oar
Were black with obols and varicoase veins
Marbled his calves and he said to us coldly:
If you want to die you will have to pay for it.

Louis MacNeice

the bones I am becoming walking off into the wind

Ken Smith

i.m
Sylvia Williams
1911 - 2011

CONTENTS

VALSE LUNAIRE

Three melancholy tramps
dancing in a ring.

Ay is the cry as they go
round and round in a wheel
and the moon
lights their dance
with silver.

Six torn coat sleeves
lift in hallelujah.
Six battered boots
thump on stone.

Ay is the cry as they jig
by the moon-stunned sea.
Three ropes of ash-grey hair
swing free.

Their bags are packed.
Their pockets sing with things.

A turpitude of tramps
capers and cries
in a ring.

Ay

ay ay

Ay

THE GOLDEN AGE OF SMOKING

Breathing the steely air
and eyeing the imperial crows,
the deer moving ever closer,
the nine towers that house

the experiment across the valley
controlled from the tallest one –
you wonder what it's for, that balcony
with the jutting concrete tongue.

Ah yes, for waving from, poised
with cigarette, a packet of ten,
Senior Service with the foil skimmed off
to disclose the untipped heads.

The foil wafts to the crowd below
who yearn for speeches with nerves
of iron, who follow, rapt, the language
of the fiery stalk that waves

at trees across the valley, the hill
you stand on, your dark shape
angry deer with antlers lowered
are surrounding. Of deep

significance, those gestures… they seem
to track the arc of your voice, those fervid
cries for HELP! you launch across the gulf
that plummet unheeded

by the smoker on his balcony.
He lights another cigarette.
The buildings throb and thrum.
Impossible projects are tearing at their heart.

What happens next? The smoker
inhales. The crowd is tense.
A faint cloud of blue perturbs
the air with silk resplendence.

ANDRÉ BRETON IN MEXICO

The *Senora* lies entombed
at the centre of her villa.
Her bedroom's long walled shut.
On the topmost floor,
shards of chandeliers
litter the ballroom tile.
Moth-chewed curtains drape
the cracked and clouded windows.
Threads of sunlight make
a quilt for cats to crouch in.
They watch a dark shape enter.
They follow the flash of a shoe.
They swish electric tails.

A girl of seventeen, bare-skinned
beneath a ragged gown of the *Senora,*
slips from out behind a screen
to scoop a favoured feline,
scattering the rest.
Her hair wound high in castles
is glossed by sun-glints from
the dusty atrium. Her brown legs
end in cherry-coloured sandals.
What has to be her name
wails down distant galleries.
She cradles purrs
and claw-thrusts of the cat.

The shoes stop. The voices fade.
Silence twists
the push and pull
of chance-empowered stares
into a double string
of cryptic braid.
She lets it go, the cat,
holds a look with hers, jet black.
Across the dance floor strewn
with shimmering débris
light transforms
a world of ruin
into a girl-filled room.

A SONG FOR THE BIRDS (FOXTROT)

Come spring the flamingoes will be gone!
In the half-built hostelry, three half-cut
bruisers jounce to trampling brass.
New wine shakes in jugs. Vines hang
down through rafters of the terrace roof.

A fractured mirror leans against the wall
to throw the heavy-footed hopping of the fat man
and the burly man in pirate braces and red hat
and the half-crazed dwarf assistant chef
at the sky. The dwarf bawls out

the fiery come-again of the refrain:
the flamingoes will be gone, come spring!
Long ago a singer wailed into a horn
to trap those words in wax. The little man
does cartwheels, handstands, backward

flips and roars he'll roast flamingo soon.
He's quite a cook, this dwarf. He'll trap
a terrapin, make you turtle goulash,
fillet snakes or barbecue a squirrel. If
spiders are your predilection, he knows

a marinade to eat them raw. The cracked old
record ends; the needle spits within its groove.
The fat man winds the clockwork, plays again
the *Sky March Threnody,* anthem of the birds,
a flying hit with revellers at carnivals

or wakes or marriages or any spry occasion
where boomps-a-daisy is required. The burly
man has had enough. He slurps a jug of wine
and flops beside the dwarf, who's cracking
snails with a spoon and potting them.

Will be gone! the fat man whoops and yells:
come spring be gone flamingoes! He's jumping
to the whoomping tuba and swigging final drops
of fresh-tapped blush. *Be gone! Be gone!*
Springo flingo, ay by jingo! Flamingoes

are a wild race, bottom-scoopers, filter-
feeders, pink as rosé wine, agents of the
Sun God. When they fly, they rassle in the air.
Come spring, the fat man bellows, *flocks of*
flame flamingoes rise in spiralling cascades!

THE BOY WHO DIDN'T MAKE IT

Too many young ones. Why was that?
They put a bench behind the rest to stand
the surplus smallies on. Wee faces peered
above the mugs of sixth-form heavies.

The man with chunky camera and tripod
addressed them all and said to try and not
put caps on back to front or make rude gestures
and not disgrace the school by gurneying.

Funnee! That had been the plan. And so
all assumed the countenances proper. Teachers
from the classrooms came and sat like blackbirds
in boards and gowns they brought out twice a year.

It was sunny and the head was smiling. At an
end of row, high upon a rear bench, stood Sam.
What Fred said now was this: If Sam jumped down
and ran like hell he'd be in the photo twice.

Sam was running before the camera moved.
He tripped and fell and lay in playground dust.
A cheer went up. Propped on scorching elbows,
he saw a wall of backs. He'd skinned his knee.

When the photo came, Sam was nowhere. From
that day on he was *Smith Invisible* and rose in-
visibly through all the classes of his education.
Now he toils with absence in a winter room –

a scratcher on a frozen windowpane, one who
publishes the frost, draws squiggles up and down
a line of the horizon, depicts a scowling eskimo,
haunts arctic fields to find the cold world's end.

Every face in that old photograph belongs to him.
Every sullen lad has raised two righteous fingers.
They've put their caps on sideways. He plans to
grimace like a dybbuk on the cover page of *Time.*

LONG ACRE

A condemned man sits in a white field.
He thinks the solitary crystal raindrop
clinging to a petal would be the perfect gift
for his executioner: a man with a wooden leg.

Far off a gallows is a-building.
Crows flock skyward at the hammering.
The executioner is trying on his hood –
though all know what he looks like.

The prisoner dreams of dashing to the stile.
In his pocket is the bent key to the missing door.
No one now will ever know his thoughts.
A wavy line ripples though the field.

The prisoner's hands are tied. They have put
a straw boater on his head and pinned to his shirt
a mugshot of the Queen's assailant.
It's not *his* face. But who's looking?

The executioner stumps up and down
practising knots. The workmen are feeding
a horse with carrots. Everyone's busy –
this might be the moment to run.

Over the stile is a field of red poppies
and a girl in a long dress reclining on a blanket.
His thoughts are like whiskers that need trimming
with a lilac-coloured barber's razor.

If he ran he would be running down
a sunlit corridor longer than the wind
that turns back on itself and back again
and twists like a knot no fingers could undo.

The executioner picks a buttonhole. He won't
bother with the hood today. No crowd.
The horse can be a witness. The workmen
have left. Shall we go? It's time.

WHAT VAN MOULDEN DID

When Van Moulden saw a chimney
he painted it. Bunched eight pots,
twin roundsels on high brick stalks,
smokeshafts advancing in helmets,
shades of ochre, red and copper,
he painted them. Pigeons
at the moment of alighting there,
two crows, their stalking shadowgraphs
across a combat zone of port-wine soldiers,
he got them down. Seven hundred fifty
canvases all told, not counting
those now lost.

The pale sun that lights his paintings,
never seen except behind an edge of cloud,
provides a wash of luminosity
over house tops stained with blood.
Deep sea creatures , dorsal finned,
rear up at gable ends above the steep-
pitched roofs of claret-coloured slate.
Crippled dwarf stacks slouch in jagged units
from here to there. Funnels thrust
against a blemished sky. Van Moulden
captured all of it, with glee.

A patron of the arts,
stepping back to get a better view,
bumps a lady on a gallery seat,
apologises,
exchanges chimney-thoughts
and goes with seven hundred pages
of catalogue he leaves with malice on a train
and smiles to think of strangers
blinking over chimney-squadrons,
distressed by that maleficent array.

Did the painter, then, foresee
the cries
of those who stare in shock
at wine-dark armies
clashed in petrified battalions
on mansards of our lives, closest to the rain?

The patron of the arts
tamps down his pipe and settles in
to watch a thriller
on TV.

STAR OF THE SEA

Maastricht, 25.x.2012

The water mill still turns
in the old town to drive the baking
of bread. Two pigeons sit
beak to beak above the wheel.

He feathers her. They fly off.
At the basilica *Our Lady of the Sea*
looks down from her shrine
on a cliff of candles that build

a wall of heat before her security
window. OK for a pagan to light one?
Someone practising the organ
falters, recovers, starts again.

I'd like to walk the ambulatory – it's
Closed to Visitors. In a city of organs,
disease is abroad. Tin plague
has devastated the pipes of St Jan.

But there's no organ in the café.
It's *Ring of Fire.* You can only sing
in the idiom they gave you, and whatever's
true is because you say it is, and if I

turn left from here instead of right
what then? Mist has gathered on
the *Maas.* The bridge goes up to let
the boats go through and down

to let the bikes across. *Technologia vincit
omnia.* Here's a bookshop in a church – what
better place for dwindling congregations?
Strollers dress for Sunday, though it isn't.

14

And yesterday the plane landed in fog.
I saw nothing but felt the bump
and we were down. This statue of the virgin –
what has it to do with the sea?

No ocean round here – a brumous canal,
a man wondering what next, cold
coming off the water. What's needed is
a guiding sound: radio for a child's ear.

I'd love to hear the blues sung free
and purged of all baroque. No candles, no
Johnny Cash, no organs – the line only,
straight as a flame, clean-edged as a die.

99 YEARS GOODBYE

April 23rd 2011

"Round the corner was always the sea." – Louis MacNeice

1

I have a deep dark dungeon feeling
and stoop to grab a piece of paper
                      the news is on
but the wind takes it and we skip
                        down the street,
me stooping, the wind grabbing it –
a little dance of stooping and grabbing.
It's too rich. It's too sweet.
The intensity bus jolts me up the hill,
drops me at electric doors that close
and open like lazy-lidded eyes.
That's enough. That'll do.
So long telling the world to behave, and it doesn't.
The willow trees are not behaving
and all the different greens of Spring
are leaping round like monkeys.
I'm drinking tea. My feet are feeling cold.
It's too sharp. It's too hot.
The Ministry of Work and Pensions called
to say you'll be a hundred. I hum
the desolate fragrance of a number.
Between a thought and words that utter it
a fish-thought hangs immobile in a tank:
tell me to stand when a lady enters;
tell me again I have a rude friend.

The news is coming. It fails to come
then comes in gouts.
I'm looking out for falling stones
that gather height and weight as they fall,
for Spring sneezes, phone calls, measurements
                                    for grave clothes.
Round the next corner you'll see it,
                        you used to say,
and we'd crane forward on the back seat...

2

Red and yellow tulips
open like lazy-lidded eyes.
Buses cruise the hill outside.
The beech tree's shadow
moves closer like a tide.

> *That'll do. That's enough.*
> *It's too rich. It's too sweet.*
> *You're looking very clean and neat.*
> *Are there many people out?*

A day that throbs with gloom.
Does anyone look neat and clean?
Down the High Road roars the echo
of a torrent through a flume –
a feral, lung-eviscerating flow.

> *I think it must be lost.*
> *It's too sharp. No, no,*
> *I've had enough. No more.*
> *Too tart. Too sour. Taste.*

A blue yacht upon the wall
has trapped her uplifted face,
a look of feeling upside down,
gone, yet winking. In a squall
the yacht leans over her bed.

Why are they putting curtains up?
We've got enough curtains. It's too much.
The orange juice is very nice.
Quite fresh. But too sharp.

Stones gather height as they fall.
Clouds leave thought adrift.
The rolling tide of shadow
gathers to obliterate
lines of mow-strip on the lawn.

It's too sharp. It's too hot.
That'll do. That's enough.
It's too rich. It's too sweet.
That's enough. That'll do.

GUSH

Come into this sunny garden
where the wasps sing and the flies buzz
where the blue hortensia is hatching a plot
where the cypress is meditating war
where the roses are intransitive and inscrutable
where the tree-stump bares all
where the vine has necrophilous yearnings
where the iron handle of the well
awaits your pump

CRACKED PIANO MUSIC

1. Sniff

I am standing on a piece of waste ground. It is Spring, full of the scents of weeds, piss, and decomposing meat. I often come here. Something may have happened in these desolate purlieus, but I don't remember what. Are those the sounds of a piano coming from below my feet?

A whiff of stale garments and humanity seeps up the stairwell of an abandoned air raid shelter. I go down the concrete steps. An old woman sprawls on a mattress under a pile of blankets and against the wall a man in a top hat sits at a no-longer upright klavier. A ray of sunlight comes through a ventilation shaft. The man is soliciting busted notes from his instrument. The tune he is trying to find will not unfold.

The woman's blue eyes are watching me. I tug away the blankets, gaze down on her bony body, then throw myself on top of her. She pretends not to have expected this and gives a little gasp of surprise. How many times have I led her down those stairs, drawing her on with words that ring with the force of my desire? Her ancient ankles lock across my back. The man in the top hat sways from side to side. He is smiling through his beard and singing a speechless song. The place grows dark; clouds pass over the sun. The woman encourages me with hoarse cries and I think: this is where it all began.

2. Legion

"In amazement we beheld the great horse." That's what they say, and they never tire of saying it, but this is not what happened at all. They beheld pigs. At first there were a few of them, their sprightly pink feet trampling over the cobblestones in haste to get wherever. No sign of a drover. We stared through windows at them. Someone had left the main gate ajar again. It was always happening. More pigs came – the pink and the less pink, the swart and the white, the spotted and the unspotted. Then came the tusked boars, big fellows with very long hair and too-sentient eyes, moving at speed and with purpose.

Where were the officers of the law? Hours passed and the torrent of pigs that had been unleashed into our streets showed no signs of diminishing. I entered the room of my father's memorabilia and took down his cavalry sabre from the wall. I buckled on the sheath, then walked to the stables at the rear. I untethered Cyclops, backed him from the stall, and mounted swiftly. I opened the heavy gates to the street and saw the river of pigs in flood. My horse whinnied and reared backward. The mob of swine had become an apocalyptic rout. I drew the blade, tightened my knees against the horse's side, crouched low, raised the sword high and shouted the command.

3. Solution

November 27th. Reading newspapers. Horse dung tipped over the Prime Minister. A dark day, much too warm. Plaster model of the heron by the artificial pond damaged by last night's wind. The crossword. *O Venus... well shalt thou know what it is to drib thine arrowes up and down Diana's leyes*. Near the effigy of itself, a live heron is pondering the terrapins – long beak versus saurian jaws, no bets on the outcome of a battle there. *One cannot assign blame for the current débacle; nobody is responsible*. Electric flickers. War in Asia. House price fluctuations. Lightning. The heron lifts off from the ground with a prehistoric wing flap and a crow swoops down from the giant cedar tree to attack it. Combat whirl above chimney tops. Thousands displaced from their homes by the fighting. The Secretary for Culture smiles at the camera through drenched hair and streaming features. Which window did the plastic bag full of urine come from? The heron vanishes over rooftops pursued by the crow.

November 28th. Rain in the night. Newspapers. Prime Minister misquoted again. Fox stalking across misty ground toward the pond; moorhens scuttle for cover. The maimed walker has completed the marathon a year late. Photograph. What chance of restoring his fortunes remains to the Prime Minister? Beak of the alabaster heron now completely awry. Someone stares into the pond. Strange-looking bird taps at the window.

November 29th. Cup of tea perched on the arm of the chair falls off. Crossword drenched.

4. Laugh

Strangers recognise me. A bearded starveling in a three-cornered hat hails me as if we had studied at college together. In the struggle of his embrace, I knock off his hat and take it with me as a reprisal, hearing his voice call after me. How does he know my name?

On the bus, I become aware of a woman looking at me from several seats away. Alighting several stops before I had planned to, I realise she is behind me. A swift click of heels on the pavement and she stands in front of me. I push her away. As she stands in a posture of supplication, another bus goes by and I spring on board.

These incidents multiply. My name is a common one, I admit, but I begin to recognise with dread the particular tone in which it is enunciated behind me. Worse than that. Strangers put their arms round my shoulders, slap my back and shout 'Gimme five!' as if for one moment I would ever have countenanced the ludicrous culture of affability to which they belong.

I take ship, move on, sail to a distant island. When the natives see me, they fall to their knees and touch their foreheads to the sand. I hear them cry 'The King has returned!' And how is it that these ladies who present themselves as wives know my carnal habits to the last trick? I lift my eyes to the volcano. Somewhere at the heart of the island is a tribe that has had no contact with the outside world. Loading two donkeys, I set out alone.

I skirt the base of the volcano and reach a wall of greenness. Naked children emerge from the foliage, followed slowly by men and women, also naked. I bow low, and trail my three cornered hat on the grass.

A man wearing a head dress of parrot feathers points at my hat and hails me by name. The watchers hail me too. They greet me with great hilarity. One laugh lights another laugh right to the end of the line. What can I do but laugh back?

A stitch cramps my side and I fall to the ground as a throng of bare feet draws closer. I look up at brown, painted faces, hundreds of them, wide open mouths, pink throats, eyes gleaming with mirth, all cheerful as hell.

5. Victory

At last our troops succeeded in breaking into the city through the southern gate. The siege had lasted 300 days and in frustration at our slow progress the Emperor often returned to his consort in the capital. Once a week, during his absence, we fired a boulder from the big catapult and rode around the walls waving our fists. The catapult was of poor manufacture; our boulders fell short. No boiling oil came down on us; we returned to our card games. My men exchanged corn and donkey meat for nocturnal visits from enemy daughters, and weapons for wine from the city cellars. I wrote to my wife that the end of the campaign was almost certainly very close.

When the wine barrels of the city were emptied and all the fertile daughters pregnant, we pushed over the heeled-up carts blocking the gateway and entered. The Emperor, brandishing his sword and accompanied by his lieutenants, rode into the main square. He howled for the slaughter to begin but our thin, lecherous army had traded in its beheading equipment and embraced the enemy instead. I sat down at a café table under some dried palm trees to study the menu. The soup was full of flavour, though the meat somewhat stringy. A carcase was turning on the spit and a delicious smell of roasting filled the air. I studied it. The donkey barbecuing in front of me might very well have been my own. The proprietor, rubbing his hands, informed me he had placed some very special red wine aside for just such an occasion as this.

6. Thoughts

Afternoon. Letting the head that is filled with disgust and hate droop on the breast. Certainly, but what if someone is throttling you? Forceful fingers have found your windpipe. How did your assailant steal so unobtrusively into the library? And to whom do they belong, these fingers? Was it something you said? Were you responsible for someone's dismissal from a well-remunerated position? Did you betray a secret, a woman? You don't even know what sex these fingers are. There is male strength in them – but the tender squeeze that is choking your airwaves reminds you of a caress.

What if this is a case of mistaken identity? It would be an ignominy to die as a result of error. Why did your attacker not check first that you are who you are thought to be? You could have exchanged pleasantries before they began their task. All that would have been visible to your assailant on entering would have been the bald spot on your crown and some wispy straggles of brown hair that are turning grey. Would it not have been advisable to compare your features with a photograph provided by an employer? And then again: what if the photo were not up to date? You have grown fat; a mole has appeared on your nose; no positive identification there. What made them seek for you in the library, anyway? You gave up the quest for knowledge long ago; the book in your lap is merely a subterfuge. What could possibly allow an enemy to conclude that you are who you are?

Such a beautiful afternoon, too. Why did you not go out ten minutes ago and leave your attacker to stalk an empty chair? Beyond the window, birds tweet and the sun is warm. Weren't you planning to take a stroll? By the children's swings in the little park, elegant mothers cross their legs and lean forward over crossword clues to which you know the answers.

Black spots appear before your eyes. There are hundreds of things you have yet to consider – and it is already too late.

7. Traces

We had set up a small fishery and built a cabin by the sea. We ignored the city at our backs, the bullet trains over the nearby viaduct, the jets that grazed our chimney stack with their wheels as they lifted for Asia. We were self-sufficient in beans, eggs, potatoes and maize. Our red cockerel guided his hens thither and back across our small acre, his head jotting hieryoglyphs of hunger on the dusty ground. The sun rose, a dirty ball of flame occluded by gases and exudations from the city. We heard their cries at night and closed our windows.

After a while came the first slither of tyres on the grassy bank above our cabin and the tread of feet down the path. They wanted to buy herring and mackerel. Having no use for money, we would solicit a garment, a jacket, a sweater, a shirt. They would gaze into the barrel of jumping silver half-moons, look at each other, and remove an item of clothing.

Years passed and our tribe grew. We took apart the cabins we had constructed, and built two boats from the planks. We harvested our seeds and placed into a cage a descendant of our cockerel and two hens. We baked our maize flour into baps, stacked our tools, and placed our agricultural records in a box. Then we hoisted the sails we had made by unstitching countless industrial garments. We had re-sewn them with triple thread into perfect triangles.

As we sailed out of the sound, I believe they kept us under observation. Inspecting what was left after our departure, they would find only vegetable plots and blank floorplans. Ahead of us, the sea stretched to the sky and the breeze was fresh in our faces. Our craft rose and tumbled through the swell. We heard the cockerel crowing and watched its ruffling comb as it stretched its neck forward and opened its beak wide to make a fanfare against the wind.

8. Speed

I am in the habit of relying on my coachman for everything. It was a struggle for him to carry the stuffed ape up to my room; the ape was unwieldy as well as heavy and my coachman is clumsy. After he had placed it near my desk, where I am writing this, I asked him to procure me a human skull. He looked surprised, then hurried off. An elderly fellow. But what is the use of an ape without a comparison?

I will have him bring the coach at four. My instruction will be simple. *To the yellow palace, Detlef, and make it snappy.* I imagine our journey with such clarity the dust of the road makes me sneeze. Detlef, high up on the box where I cannot see him, makes those cries coachmen are taught to make from an early age. The horses understand him. Beech trees and fields flash past. The vibrations of the wheels will transmit to my cheeks and belly, otherwise I lie inert across the cushions, gazing through windows at the landscape, overwhelmed by the impression of velocity. I am entirely in the hands of a man who must be eighty if he is a day. What if he has a heart attack and topples down between the shafts to be left prostrate on the road behind? The coach thunders on, the wind flying through the manes of the horses. Coming into view beyond the hills, I see the towers of the palace. Late evening sunlight catches its golden roof. I loll upon the pillows. We hurtle on.

MANTRA

Blue lagoons, crazy fires, sheaves of wheat...
A cry from the valley rises slow as smoke,
the bonfire of Autumn, heralding...what?
A wind raves then dies to livid stillness.
Footfalls tread across the grass toward
the rumoured civil wars of townships.
Thunder, now, it might be jets or the weather...

Troubadours were here, they have moved on.
Performing birds are back behind their bars.
The street rewrites itself inside your head:
smiles for shoes, and then a redfaced man
spits with fury at a whitefaced woman.
A lion prowls the jungle of its shabby cage.
Clouds bunch up in little fists of rain.

The church bell strikes against the afternoon;
shadows dance across the black of ground.
Sunlight strips the harsh ataxic highway bare,
levelling off the land, burning hilltop places dry
where butterflies and sunken earth-wasps moil.
In wooded zones away from traffic, silence
and the light stitch seamless moves together.

The distant song of hours is drowned by noise,
a biker howling in a bend with out-turned knees,
a radio that leaves the air in splinters, wrecked.
Yet still you have that little rhythm of the handkerchief
pressed and twisted in your pocket – once it's gone
you will be scrabbling, helpless on an edge:
blue lagoons, crazy fires, sheaves of wheat.

MY REAL NAME IS STANLEY KUBRICK

It was Thursday and the skeletons were out
dancing as was their custom in the beetroot
and wintry sun shone down on their fragile paleness
and earth crunched under bony feet.

No film made by actresses with bad breath
could rival their dialogues of '*Boo!*' and '*Gotcha!*'
In this film scripted by a weather forecaster
everyone misremembered their lines.

What ought to be an endearment was a whisper
disguised as a shudder that opened a creaking door
to a basement down whose cracked stone steps
skulls rolled merrily, joking as they fell.

In the house of a demented aunt, a lone skeleton
ran its clacky digit over a wrinkled forehead
and tweaked at wispy hair and put down
shadow-traps for the elderly and blind.

It was Midnight in the garden of the beetroot
and the skeletons went down one on the other
and tasted each other's bones like crows pecking
chicken carcasses, or directors filming mud.

THE DREAMER AWAKES

The music in the tomb is sweet,
a syrup of oblivion. The faces of the gone
lie clearer etched on polished stone.
One who'd always trouble sleeping
stretches perfectly reposed. And her?
That laughing woman who dreamed and saw
her dream surprised by fate – have all
the restless accidents that marked her
smoothed into a look that sees forever?

The music of the pharaohs, eastern banjo,
tambourine and sticky clarion, uncoils
a darkness in the mind that descends
a narrow stairway skewed through walls
of sandstone to a dome-roofed chamber
where water streams around a slab
to which the dreamer comes like one
who knew there'd be a taper burning here.

A rattle and a thump – the portcullis
falls to close the vault. The dreamer looks
around. Manes of horses stream in white
cascades; servants wait for orders;
a lion lifts a rugged paw and halts;
the smell of an asphyxiating flame
comes reeking on a gust of wind that
should not gust, and does not, any
more than dreamers breathe on mirrors.

The lion's roar gives vent to silence.
The dreamer gazes up at hieryoglyphs
that tile the curving roof. No way to tell
his thoughts, if he is re-acquainting
memory with light that follows dark.
Across the veil of time waft drifting threads.
Last hope: to be not talked about.
What world is this, that ending does not end
and leaves the dreamer with that smile?

WELCOME TO THE MULTIPLEX!

1. Episode in Santa Candela

Louisa Dreed, daughter of
Elijah Dreed, the Cornflour King,
is found smearing herself
with the blood of children.
Did Louisa do the slicing?
Hank Droneboom, psychiatrist,
puts her in a tower of glass.
She plays with kewpie dolls,
with rubber knives and plastic hammers.
Slice follows thump follows slice.
When she undresses at night,
Don Speke, the Hollywood detective,
studies the V of shadow
between her smooth-waxed legs.
A leopard and lily relationship
grows between minder and patient.
Has Droneboom not revealed
in *The Leopard and the Lily*
how the deep pulls you under?

On hot days, Louisa rides
a little train that carries her
up and down the glassy ramps
of the Humphrey Bogart tower.
The dirty old sun descends;
Louisa rides her freight car back.
She's making choo-choo noises,
watched by Hank and Don.

She pouts at Don in passing.
He's paid for keeping watch, not smiling,
but dollars cannot calm
the snare-drum of his heart.
He wears the tired look
redundant film stars have;
his watch is like a dream,
his dream is an eternal pause.
Certified for vigilance
by the Motion Picture Guild
for Conformism, Authority, and Distribution
he falls asleep on the job.
Hank's toothy smile is very Dutch.
Watching on a cyberlink,
he's awake in Amsterdam.

At three in the morning
she tiptoes in
where Don lies dreaming in his cot.
What price minding now
when sweet Louisa straddles
him with open daycoat and he
with a battery heart im-
planted by the Movie Surgeon General?
To kiss that psychotic belly
will risk the furniture and himself
but away into the parking lot they run
and soar to the darkening west.
Stop! she cries *You're mine!*
and breaks him up with a bouncy hammer,
dismembers him with a moody knife.
Her father waits at the Fortune Motel;
they feed Don's ghost to the breeze.

In a fiscal flash, Dreed's on the phone:
"She's cured, Hank. The francs are in the bank."
"What about Don? Did he die?"
"He'll go into the concrete, Hank.
He's gonna be the final heave
in my Bridge of the Enduring Sigh."

Theme tune.
Snores of the audience,
Cries of an old lady being eaten alive by cinema termites.
Lights.

2. Mouthsville USA

At the OK Coral Island Gas Station, just off the beach,
(Prop. Jim Palmtree)
Jim is filling the tank of an old Chevrolet.
Time-fuel, cheapest of all, it gets you there
before you left, no need to drive at all.
Nice day, says the motorist, what's up?
You're the first customer, says Jim, in seventy years,
                              where you been?
I tell you, Frond, says the customer,
we was all evacuated when the volcano blew.
Ah, says Jim, I stayed for that. Didn't want no evacuation.
Hole opened up behind my kitchen
                        wider'n the Grand Canyon,
but no smoke, no fire, no lava. Just steam.
How so, Frond?
Well, says Jim, it was the Magma Time Giant hisself.
See that opening there – that was his mouth –
and out of that mouth came words.
That so, Frond?
And being as I was right here – I heard 'em:
words from before and after ourselves,
both ways into the middle, I'd say,
and mighty clouds of steam to boot.
To boot, Frond?
Steamed up so you couldn't look through 'em –
word visibility zero. But they gave me pause.
They did?

Pause to look at them houses perched
around the giant's teeth –
old people seated in the dark
drinking dark liquors, thinking thoughts
                              darker'n darkness,
and the cock not crowing at the back of it all,
stupid old cock, doesn't know what time it is,
doesn't crow at all.
That's what it said? the customer asks.
Didn't say it, says Jim. Steamed it though.
And then it went back down the hole
leaving a whole lot of spare time
I'm just trying
to use up.
You're a thrifty fellow, the customer says,
but if that's the case, think I'll
stay evacuated. Bye bye.
And the Chevrolet vanishes too
and four shiny hub caps
roll round the forecourt in a wheely dance
followed by Jim, tap-tapping after them,
skipping over trails of phantom time-fuel
that darken cement with ghostly spittle.
And the grey-black lips of the thrown-open mouth
grow wider apart under hot blue sky
where tides gnaw the bay
bite after bite
after bite.

3. A Town Called Anger

Midge Dauntless walks out
on her crap job in Anger
and tramps through the town
where waves pound the harbour
and encounters Shagg Pony
in a rain-whipped shelter
and straightway she falls for
the cut of his jib
the trim of his spinnaker
the snarl of his voice holding thrills of the sea
and she loosens the clip on her blouse.

On the way into town,
riding Shagg Pony's Vespa,
they pass a parked Volvo
where Silas van Beukel
is fondling the leg
of Derek, his helper,
who stifles his boss with his keys.
From Huddlesea Heights,
out on a balcony,
Lalia Whisper
trains her new telescope
on a man she sees tugging
at the end of legs.
What a splash! What a swirl! What a plunge!
She swings to the bedroom
with thrills in her heart.
Has Peepee popped his Viagra?
He snores under bedclothes.
She raises her telescope
and brings it down hard
on slumbering Peepee's skull.

At Loanshark & Mutual
the alarm bell is ringing.
Midge revs the Vespa outside.
With gold in a bag, Pony leaps out
and Derek roars by in the Volvo.

What a gust! What a breeze! What a smash!
Pursued by a Vespa ridden by Venus
the vanishing Volvo speeds
till it comes to a halt
in the Valley of Tears
and Derek invites her
to view the Volvo's inside.

Up the thin streets of Anger
walks Lalia Whisper
seething with unthanked desire.
In the treasure-chest-open
eyes of a dead man
she glimpses fathoms of gold.
Far from the town
upholstery creaks
and Midge breathes red leather
and Derek becomes a man.
The wind thrashes flags
and washing lines jitter
and Lalia leans
on the rail of the pier.
She's calling a name to the storm.
Who is she calling? Who can it be?
What a take! What a cut! What a fade!

The clouds cruise the sky
and the dead take their bows
and Silas and Peepee roll
and the fire of the tide
moves the shadows below
in synch
with the shadows above.

THE SEA BRIDGE

for Elke

Every day he walks its length,
a mile of dunes and mud flats to the sea.
The planks are broken now, railings
sagged or fallen. Half way out a kink
in its trajectory holds high-backed benches
that once protected walkers from the wind,
a place to sit and contemplate the gulls.
No sitting now. Damaged slats will poke
you in the back or rip your clothes. But
walk a little further, a crumbling hut
awaits its visitors; trouser-polished seats
give respite from a sheet of hail or
shelter from an arctic winter wind.

He's stopped bothering to take the fee
from visitors although he greets them
with a cry of pleasure whether company
or not is what they seek. He leads them
out along the bridge, identifying
pipers, terns and curlews, throwing
wide his arms to show the one idea
that goads him: horizon. What other
measure gives a truer feel of near and far?
No nasty alp, be sure of that. Across the
perfect flatness his hands describe a slow
synoptic sweep. In torrents he deplores
the broken-downness of his charge.

At the water's edge, a quarter mile away from
where the sea bridge ends, on rusting iron legs,
stands the ruin of the pleasure palace: *Noah's Ark.*
Once they came from counties all around,
rode along the boards in pony traps
for roaring evenings high above the weather,
came clacking back by torchlight, women

squealing, men in sly umbrageous moods.
He blows his nose and leans upon his broom.
Today the Ark is leaning more than usual.
Last night's storm ripped yards of railing
from the bridge. Thin clouds are trailing now
at length across the pastel-coloured sky.

How long he broods across the sweep
he doesn't know. No life of moments could
be longer. With cracking sounds like rifle fire
the pillars of the Ark begin to fall. Its structure
warps, it hangs and crashes to a heap of bones.
It seems to breathe – but waves beneath
are causing it to rise and fall. He sees it happen.
His mind repeats it. He feels the shuddering planks.
They're a hazard now, the bridge is dangerous.
And with ocean suddenness the clouds crash
over him; thunder hurls its rattle round the sky.
Rain-blooms, wind-borne, flash against his face.
When the gale hits nine, he starts to sing:

Ten green bottles, hanging on the wall!
If one green bottle should accidentally fall…!
He tilts his voice against the blast; each
squall attacks the words and drags them off.
Mad dogs, he thinks. Arousal of the sea
brings hordes of them. He can see what's coming
from its distance, always coming…*Five green bottles…!*
There are waiters hurling tablecloths, swinging
four-branched candelabra. Lightning strikes
 the fun pavilions, howling diners snap their fingers
for the final bill…And there'll be gusto for the sauce:
No green bottles hanging on the wall..!

HAMPSTEAD FAIR

i.m. Ben Sutton

You were a devilish handsome fellow, Ben,
with your mechanical leg and dirty laugh.
Sailing up into the night, the Big Wheel took us
to the highest point and then broke down.

You scared me, rocking at our seat, much too
wild for me to be amused. I thought we'd jump
our fragile axle. The seat restraints were loose.
Ghostly pinprick faces stared at us from safety.

Now I slip into the crowd, looking for the tent.
I don't expect to find her, don't recall her name.
A sign reads: 'Donna Bella: Oriental Seer' –
If your love is hidden, I will tell you where.

She's been promoted to a caravan. On a copper tray
I drop a crumpled note. She takes my hand
in long, bejewelled fingers, bends her kerchiefed
head toward my palm. "Sit down young man."

Come off it, Donna – but I sit. If that crystal ball
were shaken, would it snow? She may not be
as old as she might want to look. Mumbo jumbo first,
in gypsy, then: "You call yourself a poet" – that

gets my full attention – "yet I find no rainbows
in your poems, no sunsets. How often do you stand
and look at stars?" "When the lights go out," I say
"but this is cloudy country." She meets my eyes.

"Are you Leo or Aquarius? In your poems, I do not find
a world I recognise. Tell me, do you know this man?"
I gaze into her crystal ball; a figure seems to swirl in fog.
Above her head, a mirror framed in light bulbs gleams.

"Once," she says, "this person longed for fire-struck
words to throw a brightness at the world." I nod. That
covers nearly every one. Witches always have a half truth
that fits all. Maybe she thinks it might apply to me?

But the crystal clarifies a vagueness in my mind.
A feeling as of someone that I know who tries and fails
to reach me makes me frown. Then she plays the joker's
card: her voice enacts a chuckle building to guffaws.

"His laugh exactly! How did you do that?" The mirror
flashes. "Yes, your friend. The reason you are here, no?
He died last year in Greece." Her head scarf seems to
twinkle; her face is shrouded underneath: "But that's

impossible," I say, "you never met my friend." "Indeed, I did
not have the pleasure. You paid to enter, did you not, young man?
Look up, look up at stars." The mirror drinks its ring of gleams.
My lips move, word-dull, through the glitters of that silver pool:

"There's nothing in the stars for me," I say. "That cousin witch
of yours told my friend he'd lose his other leg. This star sign crap
is bad for mental health. Her voodoo screwed him, put a jinx on him
forever." The gypsy tracks my lifeline with a finger:

"That may be so. I see the power of my sister's divination
never left you. But why let moments high in darkness
chill your memory? Let the wheel of fortune turn again
and bring you down. Imagine you're still there… decide

in your descent that you will grasp the world, not let
it slip away. Your friend awaits your choice. He says…"
her eyes are shadow-lights "… the spirit world is poised
on your behalf." She exits through a curtain. I sit,

unmoving; the fires inside the crystal ball recede.
Getting up, I hear the floor protest. The trailer rocks.
I creak toward the door, go down the steps into the crowd.
Up the hill, the inch-arounding wheel is bathed in light.

41

INFECTED MOMENT

for Gizi

No cure for the double doom exists
it struts like a typewriter, writes the unspeakable
mutters *blood! blood!* in a tin-foil voice
shuts the door and locks it, with you inside

It crawls into the smile of the dark-haired woman by the pool
and occupies her nervous system, balance itself
dives off the see-saw straight to the O of her mouth –
a gymnast-curver high above a smash

No current stirs the waters of the Double Doom Hotel
except for the mincing of the damned by the cutlery trolley
except for the parasols shutting their eyes to the blindness
and the dripping thing that lifts its head above the sill

But for the creaking and clinking of her synapses being demolished
the prowling of snorkels down the lanes of her twenty-two years
the green flux that eats her, the tiles that speak in dog
she'd warn the silence, fill the empty spaces with her roar

Thirteen detonation-counting doctors sit
in closet-privacy with fix-u-nothing smiles
a voice declares the double doom your order sir hello
consultancies explode in mirror-popping shards

'Jump!' shout the medics, *'Swim for it! Go!'*
and roll their tinctures and punctures across the floor
and summon the weeping poker players in masks
'Play out the hand!' they call *'Deal!'*

But the last hand is the one that is dealt too soon
it brings the sky in a bucket to the O of her eyes
brings across the patio with careful steps the gleam
that the double doom downs with a quaff and a hiccup and burp

VILLAGE MUSIC

after Johannes Bobrowski
Dorfmusik

Final boat on which I stand
with no hat and tangled hair
riding four white boards of oak
and a rue-sprig in my hand
friends are walking to and fro
    someone plays the trumpet
    someone plays trombone
boat go well and keep afloat
others strike a whispered note:
that one built on sand

From the well-pole calls the crow
from the branchless tree *alack*
from the bark-stripped perch a croak:
take away that rue bouquet
take away that posy
    now there sounds a trumpet blast
    a blast on the trombone
no one comes to take my spray
time won't have me back they say
I have not far to go

So I know and here I sail
with no hat and tangled hair
moonlight round my eyes and beard
life lived foolish to the end
catching once a high-up wail
    a ringing of that trumpet
    a bray of that trombone
the crow is calling from afar
I am where I am: in sand
with the rue sprig in my hand

THE THEORY OF GRAVY

A squawking poem in memory of Pee Wee Russell

"No one familiar with the characteristic excitement of his solos, their lurid, snuffling,
   asthmatic voicelessness, notes lent on till they split, and sudden passionate
   intensities, could deny the uniqueness of his contribution to jazz." – Philip Larkin

It is so very hard
to get the rudeness of a wallop in your line
to find the rusty nails to make uneven hammered joints
to trap the incivility sublime.
Let us now upturn
the bucket of the unpredictabilities
and stand a crowing chanticleer on its rim.

Imagine first a train.
Now imagine it a clarinet.
It flutes a little as it leaves the station.
Its wagons play a tune of stops
on walls of cherry-weathered brick.
How glad you are
you thought you caught this train!

You are steaming, let us say,
or puffing, or chuffing, or piping or wailing along.
What threads attaching to the world are those
that clank behind us!

Your train that whistles to the far horizon
is loaded up with gravy.
Its engineers sing of it with
insufflating panic
and you are feeling sad and happy both at once.

Behold the power of the gravy rising up
to spread the yearning and the glory thin
through wrong notes hit repeatedly
till Pee Wee gets them right!

And yet you missed this train.
Everyone aboard has missed it.
The gravy has departed with the train;
its absence is expounded
in yelps and self-destructive quavers –
what a figment all this is! –
and far away
offloaded by a smiling wagoner
beyond the confines of a classic song
the gravy rests.

THE KIRMES PARADE

The flies are devoted to this appassionata.
The church-tower has magnetised the mob.
Nothing but jugglers, stilt-walkers, flame-spitters,
the thrashed bells' lingering throb.

Witchcraft's what we need. A diabolic rite
to drive those plangent discords out,
repulse those clonkings from the spire, give
that consecrating caterwaul a clout.

Once it was a horse fair. What could make
more sense than that? You'd throw
a noose across a wild horse and trade it.
But sense lived seven centuries ago.

All my life they told me I was lazy.
I failed to rise at four and tiptoe to my desk.
I hated where the words were taking me –
deep into the picturesque.

I should write here snuggled up in bed with you,
and scribble rhymes upon your skin.
I need to flay that poppycock parade
and launch a vengeful boogie at its din.

The bedroom's being killed. It shakes
and writhes. Books fall off the shelves.
Your gaze arraigns me. The roof's gone crazy.
The racket splits us into selves.

Outside, on sticks, they're holding cherubs up.
Surplices and smocks! When dark creeps in
they'll violate the cherubs with roars
of swooping melody they call a hymn.

How that lewd procession clunks!
Angels wobble. I sense them as they come –
tense young men with futures in their fists,
whacking out their names upon a drum.

FLASHES

d'aprés Jean-Arthur-Nicolas Rimbaud, relâché

Five 'Illuminations' for the taste of the day.

1. Landspit

Darkened gold and shimmering evening give rise to the brick of new estates that rear above themselves; they throw out a spit of land as large as a knees-up in Poland, or the great eel of Japan, or the west of the middle east. From the fanatics who put torches in the school uniforms of theory that open up immense panoramas for the defence of modern ideas; from painted panjandrums with their hot flushes and savage orgies; from giant Carthaginian marquees for the bankrupt wedding parties of alcohol-dependent Venice; from the shapely outflows of Etnas; from the crevices in giant females and the shouts for help from Fox's glacier mints; from the toilets surrounded by tall Germans; from the remarkable pork trawlers who perch on the tops of the trees of Japan, and the obese shapes of knobs and tiaras from Scarborough or Brooklyn; from their railways that outflank, arch over and bore through the sofa-like postures chosen by history to outdo the most complex and highly-inflected grammatical forms of Italy, America or Asia, whose mighty case endings and tearaway donkey subjunctives are known as 'dawn gliders' or 'barrage balloons' or 'ripe farts'; from the open vodka bottles of travellers and toffs – that which allow wild side-slapping dances by the whores of the moment – and even down to the voltage of illustrated art valleys where vast apple-corers hollow out the brains of those undergoing beauty treatments, welcome to the appearance of honesty in Landspit.

2. Translated

Reality is too much like spinach for my enormous ego, – however, wearing a greasy eagle outfit I found myself feathering a dame. howling verses at the ceiling and beating my wings over her storm-clouded nightdress.

I became the hoof of a bald horse holding up her physical delicacies, those much-loved baubles, and then a vulgar bear with violent jaws, white-haired with regret, then a silvery consolation with glittering eyes.

We were in a boiling fish tank, tooting sombre suffusions.

Come morning – rioters were trying to burn the joint down – I had turned into an ass, and I ran through the streets with a pulsating hard-on, braying, until the local housewives dragged me on to their bedsprings.

3. Carrying a Torch

To my sister Louisa van Driver of Vobster: She blows a trumpet for northern motherhood. – No more questions!

To my sister Libby Abwood of Abbot's Abbas. Wow! – the rolled up and sumptuously scented spliff. – To the liberation of mothers and children.

To Lulu – show-off – she suffers from gout after the drinking parties of her friends that stopped her finishing her degree in Oratory. To obnormal amnivores. – To Madame Asterisk.

To the lunatic I was. To this dilapidated tramp with a mission to emigrate.

To methylated spirits. To a clergyman on a pole.

Let me not forget those people who go to Stonehenge at the solstice and organise the events that demand your *entire* participation, polished, serious, vices in which you pursue the vacuum cleaner of the moment.

Tonight though, to Clarissa of the elevated reflections, fat as a pussycat, lit up like ten months at the Red Night Inn – (she's a sucker for conserving spunk), – to my one dumb muffin, my fly-by-night who keeps one jump ahead of bother boys more violent than intercourse between bears.

To all those pricks, whatever they smelt like, even those imaginary puff puff games. – And that's *it*.

4. Democracy

The flag marches across the stinking landscape; and our gibberish stuffs the trombone.

"We will centralise and service the most swanlike prostitution. We shall put loathsome logic to death.

"Book us a package deal! We'll squirt your cucumbers for you! – we'll bring the gorillas to fleece you, the new hotels and the security hard men.

"A good goodbye to anyone here, I don't care who. We're recruiting ourselves. We're cooking up a death ideology; knowing nothing of anything, we'll service excess; let the world croak, it deserves to. That's progress. Forward, march!"

5. Genius

He's the infection of now. He lets in the scum of winter and the stew of summer. He's the one who has baptised our food and drink. He captures the delicious taste of tram stops and puts the evil eye on places that try to escape. He's the now of the future, the power and the orgy. Those of us left to express our rage by insane head-on collisions with trouble see him whizzing overhead in a whirlwind of orgasmic flags.

He's coupling itself, re-calculated and redrawn, an unpredictable planner of miracles, not to mention eternity: that machine you esteem for its fortune-telling trapdoors. You have to admit his knot-tying power: he makes a joke of our sanity, runs away with our universities; feverish, super-sensitive Egyptian pasha that he is, he's dangerous to get drunk with, – he has unfinished business with alcohol.

We rap him over the knuckles and he's off…And when the church-going stops, he yells loud warnings: 'Behind the superstition of your ageing bodies there is nothing but circuses and traditions. The century is going dark!'

He isn't angry, he's not coming down off his ladder, he's not going to carry any woman's shopping or furnish fun for the boys; he's gone fishing, driving that suicidal car, full of amens.

What scuffling, what sulking, what shopping sprees: the terrible completeness with which falling stocks and shares gather speed.

What fruity vodka! How incomprehensible it all is!

His body! the hip pistol, the truculent prayer, novel kinds of violence on the cross!

His pictures, – photographs of ancient kneelings down and whippings! He pisses all over them in his hotel room.

His timetable! the cancellation of musical insults, the removal of sound-waves for the most intense music of all – silence.

His pacing-up-and-down! Departures vaster than any mere arrivals.

It's either him or us! Bees in the organ loft or timeless charlatans.

Hear the moans and the moonlight chanting! the sudden accidents!

He cheated us all and we thought OK, if the cap fits on a winter's night, wear it, from the tumbling down flagpoles on the castle to the idiots with the diseases, from the polite glances to the lascivious gropings, from the phone calls to the executions, whether pegged out under the incoming creep of the tide or in front of the galloping hooves of approaching horses, do what he says, follow his shuffling dance, his body, his light.

THE CLASSIC DOUBLE-TAKE

That was me, up on the roof again
sitting above the houses and the sea
reading a book of misbegotten love.
Below me, bird-crapped, was the spire
of the church and a crane, not swinging
(it was Sunday) and bikes with human
cargoes dawdled on the dike beside the beach.
To my twisty tale I'd closed my eyes
when a seagull carnival of noise
caused me to open them and see

a man walking in from the sea
with a rolling stride that made a noise
of thunder louder than surprise.
Taller than a steeple, broader than a beach
but unmistakably human,
he'd arms like power station chimneys, swinging,
and kicked up waves to crash against the spire,
and bellowed out a dungeon song of love
in baritones that soared to hit High C.
I glanced. And then I very slowly looked again.

A FESTIVAL

It makes you want to weep: the drum of years.
Down the street toward the ocean, on the plaza
at the end, fourteen circling dancers, arms inter-
linked, spin to fast accordions and taradiddles from
a motley-clad percussionist who calls out: "feel
your feet and weave the ring!" A gypsy with a Fender
bass, four gold teeth and feather-studded hat
provides the underpinnings, devil-droning thumps.

A crowd has formed beneath the city's plane-trees.
Locals, jostlers, eager pocket-pickers, beggars, men
on crutches, wheelchair-folk with smiling handlers
jig to glad but broken-hearted music. A clown-faced
singer with a sad and smiling mouth and mad-as-
mutton hair sports a smock with giant buttons.
He mounts the rostrum with a bound of joy
to warble blithe-blue lyrics at a yellow microphone.

Standing high above the dancers and the band
he pays fantastic court to Columbine beneath
the sulky-browed cathedral on Founder's Rock:
throw away the gum of tears! let weeping die!
If sadness could be funny, he'd be priceless.
If humour could be tragic, he'd be Shakespeare's thumb.
The gypsy's fingers fly along his fretless fretboard
pressing glum fandangoes from the off-tuned strings.

Now the dancers gather speed as the drummer
blows a whistle, clips his hi-hat zish-staccato…
The singer yodels: *sweep away the the years…!*
The gypsy's amp reverbs an oriental hum…
In the high cathedral's tower, a blank-faced beadle
oils his crossbow, fits a quarrel to the stock, draws
a bead upon the singer's open mouth and waits
to hear the phrase: *now's the time to drum…!*

The beadle lets his crossbow rip. The bolt goes down
the singer's throat, who holds the note and ululates:
the leaping spears have come! He crashes to his knees.
The crowd's amused. Then someone shouts 'Assassin!'
Sadness forms a cloud; gaiety turns numb. Dancers
scatter, the drummer thuds, accordionists are
fleeing, but the gypsy plays arpeggios of steel:
no fears! he roars! *feel the power of my thrum!*

A DREAM OF KOS

Looking up I see a grove of olives.
My rear view mirror shows me cows
on the road. A car-smashing pothole
may be next. Then I see the taverna.
Its sign is an hourglass with neon sand,
flowing. My hand is held fast

and Dimitri asks do I propose to fast
or will I join him in a feast of olives?
He winks and points to the white sand
on the beach where a pair of cows
are swimming out to sea. His taverna
is for stories and jokes and potholes

deeper than the ordinary potholes
that merely swallow tourists. Breakfast
means sunshine in this lyrical taverna.
It means accepting the proffered olives
and believing that what swims is cows.
'Don't think that's merely sand

you can see,' Dimitri says, 'that sand
is time. It is also bottomless potholes
you must dodge like foot-trampling cows
and it causes your life to rattle fast
but you can slow the flow by thinking olives
and sit at the bar in my taverna.'

Over the church floats a cloud taverna
and little white shrines. Cockerels and
half-built hotels line the route of the olives
and taxis waylaid by wandering potholes
find a shower of pumpkins bouncing fast
off their bonnets. In a field I see cows

languidly munching weeds and cows
scratching necks on sky-blue tavernas
and I'm driving a long straight road too fast
while the cops stick traffic boards in sand
to show the depth of those potholes.
I give 'em the finger: *Mind the Olives!*

(Huh!) *Cows on the Road! Silting Sand!*
One Taverna can Conceal Another Pothole!
I'm fastening my star to those olives.

THE SWIMMING POOL AT TÖNNING

Behind the dam across the Eider river
the estuary is three miles wide. A great
construction bars the flood of North Sea tides
that batter at its iron gates. Upstream,
seals slump on sandbanks, sheep graze meadows
lusher than the saturated sky; Arctic Tern
bring fish catch to their young. Continue
on the dike path by the river till
the twisted spire of Tönning hoves in view.
You can take a mudbath here, wade
into the rich absorbing wallow, feel
your feet glide in, the brilliant slough
accept you. For those whose temperament
abjures a slosh, a swimming pool invites.
Salty water, blue and filtered, awaits
your jump. Got your spa card?
Taxes paid? Dive in. Get wet. Enjoy.

You're not the only swimmer. Observe
that white-haired man of eighty swim two lengths
then stop to trade an insult and a joke
with the lady who is lifeguard and cashier
and server at the café counter where
the choice is several sorts of ice
or a plastic beaker full of acid coffee.
Fourteen and chubby, half-submerged,
two girls practise kissing mouth to mouth.
A gang of boys is laughing, though at what
it's hard to say. From the highest diving board
more lads hurl themselves into the water;
as one goes down another takes a run

and follows, missing him by inches.
The lifeguard screeches from her windowed cubicle
but boys like jumping, girls like
kissing; the sun dictates from zenith.

On a bench three ladies sit and sip
their blood-undoing brew, and talk, and talk.
There's more to talk about in Tönning
than you might think. A man in jeans
and T-shirt, his brown arms dense with wiry hair,
the tip of a baroque tattoo just visible
between his shirt hem and bravado belt,
stops to add a little to what's said and
everyone is laughing. There's a lot to laugh at
here in Tönning. Conspiracies
unravel while you plough your furrow
back and forth; your head bobs up with
every stroke in time to catch what follows.
Good thing you thought to bring your goggles,
somewhat smeary, true, but through them
you see faces changing with the voltage of surprise
to hear the school director and a pupil have eloped.

You've nearly done your twenty lengths.
You like this town. You like its photogenic mayor,
his squint-eyed deputy who's clearly hatching plots,
the business plans of lawyer Hollergreve.
You admire the bearded benefactor's bust –
the man who built the pool in 1927
and founded Tönning Swimming Club and built
the fine hotel. The posters in the lobby for
the long departed circus and the pastor's fund
to cure the spire's kink engage your revery.
You feel a kinship with the passion of the skinny youth
who dreams of leaving Tönning and doesn't realise
the girl beside him has got plans for him
and all of this beside a river full of mud,
incomparable, shiny, slicky, health-bestowing mud,
that curves into a distance live with gulls,
three miles wide across, gleaming under heaven.

REDS

My painful duty, comrades —
I shall not spare you from the truth —
is to expose the so-called grace
of the creature with a tail as big as itself.
We denounce its sense of humour!

We shall not flinch from spelling out
the words 'atrocity' and 'wisecrack.'
That bouncing beech nut on your head
is flagrantly a covert operation.
These bourgeois jokes must cease!

Its dance on any garden trellis-work
is nothing less than infamous subversion.
Note the swaggering rump, the cocky to-and-fro.
Another walnut tree planted in your border?
This provocation must be punished!

They chase pigeons from our trees,
pursue our magpies over roofs!
Shall we stand idly by and let them leap
and grab a bending twig and swing there?
Must branches bow to an oppressor's weight?

We must protect our trees.
Fell them! Fell them! Let clearances
prepare a country free of verticals.
Eradicate this hollow ginger wit
of quips, unseemliness and flashing tails!

Let there be no more communiqués
from the world of flying high resolve.
Evict these twinkly braggarts from their platforms!
Cleanse the tallest perches of pseudo-ideology!
No more clinging to a branch that's bound to break!

We must introduce the market trader grey.
It will feed from outstretched hands.
It prefers the ground to trees. Act now to end
the grind of teeth on fabulous lofty nuts!
Silence that chomping on the really significant cones!

RIDE

This Donkey Five Quid read the sign.
I brought the car to a squealing stop.
No, said my wife, we don't need a donkey.
It's only five quid! I said. We've no room,
she said. It's the bargain of a lifetime, I said.
Where will you put it? she said. In the
garage, I said. And where will you put
the car? she said. Who needs a car, I said

when you have a donkey? They need
to eat, she said, you have to feed them.
It can eat the lawn, I said. We have no lawn,
she said, you ruined it. Long story short,
I walked up to the big house, paid a fiver.
How will you get it home? said my wife.
I'll ride it, I said, like Sancho Panza, and I
climbed on. It didn't move. Gee up, I said.

It still didn't move. I bet, said my wife,
it never goes anywhere. I bet the owner
sells it to everyone who goes past. See that
flash? He's watching you through glasses.
Come on, Eeyore, I said. Do me a favour.
It didn't move. It stared at my wife's blouse.
OK, I said, we'll tie the rope round its neck
to the bumper. That's cruel, she said, and

anyway you don't have a bumper, this car
is all in one piece. I said: Lower the windows
and tie the rope to the middle pillar, this
donkey needs exercise. She started the engine.
Over the turnip field we slid till the rope snapped.
Look, said my wife, you've bent the car.
It was bent already, I said. No it wasn't, she said.
I hung back the sign, walked to the house

and bashed the front door till my fists hurt.
Hysterical laughter came from within. Behind
came a crunching of hooves on the gravel.
Well, well, said my wife, you've made a new friend.
Eeyore! I said. It stared at my green trousers.
My wife, who was knee deep in ferns, gave a
slow handclap. The house went asylum quiet.
We clopped home in a gang like a circus.

SPECIES

The marabou-poet-bird
looks senatorial, except for the eyes,
those scrutinising beads that follow you about.
They do follow you about.
Might you be lunch?
No such luck.

From time to time
the marabou-poet-bird makes an attempt
at flight. Crossing the ground
in a jumping run like rocket-man trying to take off
it stops before it hits the fence
to consider a shabby palm.

The thoughts
of a marabou-poet-bird
are heavy with complications.
They are, quite frankly, a deterrent to flight.
Prizes on the ground absorb it –
the kind gathered up with a snap.

But marvel at the way this stately brooder
on thoughts too deep for flying
sprints across its enclosure
when the food pail tips in its trough.
Do flashes of humour ever penetrate
the gravity of this melancholy soul?

Absolutely not.
Watch how it stands on one leg
and droops its beak, examining its foot.
The foetid water it is standing in
reflects a face that holds it spellbound.
One thought is spinning in its head:

Come little Muse! Clack!

PEAK

He'd brought his *pic à glace*
    for the ice that gripped the col,
a game of whist to while away
      his fear of altitude,
and held up to the light
      a glass of Bordeaux wine
he pecked from on a boulder,
      staring down the view.

From slopes of the ravine,
      the black sheep baa-ad
His voice unlatched by alcohol
    baa-ad back until they stopped.
Plucking out his knapsack pack,
    he dealt himself a hand of solitaire.
Would the bottle last? Did he really care
      if he didn't make it to the top?

No way they'd know
      if he reached the summit
to bury in the snow
    the empty bottle of *Merlot*
or raised the flag of the republic
      whose citizen he wished to be.

Still, what counted
    was the silent will to speak.
The pock-marked alp alone
    would see what card he picked.
He cut the deck and sighed:
      another *As de Pique*.

ASTOUNDING TROUSERS

It was very dark in Gabriel's pockets, where he kept his hands as he strode along. His hands curled and uncurled like fronds in an aquarium.

He followed the gaudy trousers without realising what he was doing. Their flaring filigree diverted him from his direction. What hypnotic material were they made of? It was some kind of corduroy, patterned in vertical swathes of zebraic orange and foxy yellow. He turned left into Coptic Street when he should have gone straight ahead.

So often trousers enclose peg-legs, crutches, bony hobbledehoys. Not these. The curves of the seat fell, rose, balanced on sweet afflatuses and then decorously wobbled down each side of a paradisal hill to come soaring up again and declare roundness. They concealed a mystery in order to reveal it. Like any naturalist, Gabriel felt himself magnetised by their wake. Dodging pedestrians, he leapt stag-like in pursuit as the rounds before him swayed on – exquisite tightrope walkers crossing an abyss.

Trousers. The way they cupped the future with each tense swerve of reciprocity to the human material made him hunger with thirst. He needed a drink. It would be the moment to enter a shop with two descending steps, push open a door, and cause a bell to ring in some distant room. After a long while a gentleman in shirt-sleeves with eye-shade pushed up, having possibly quit a game of poker being played in the back, would enter to describe a year, the slopes of a vineyard, the proximity of the vineyard to the sea, the characteristic of a particular grape. They would stand together sipping an ancient vintage and be spectators of silent children dancing in a ring. Gabriel would grasp the ring with both hands and shrink it to a glittering halo. Walking to the cliff edge of the vineyard and tossing it down, he would glimpse a salmon leaping to swallow it. Naturally it would be found by a girl at the fish counter, a golden band she would later slide on her finger, transforming herself into a goddess.

He would feel himself *vielli en fûts de chêne*.

The man in shirt-sleeves would refill their glasses. He would raise his own glass and then plunge a dagger into his eye. With the hilt protruding, he would continue to tell the wine's story: how huge estates had been lost on the turn of a card in a poker game before the war; how tremendous vintages had been dispersed; how thunderstorms and disease had destroyed the harvests. Gabriel would nod slowly, staring at the streaming, bifurcated visage before him, grasp the cobwebbed bottle and walk out from the shop onto barren slopes, furious rain, lightning and darkness. He would seek refuge from the wild weather of his mind in a shepherd's hut.

66

Of course she would be there. Why in a world of misfortune should the figure of his imagination *not* await him there in eye-seductive trousers? She would undress and Gabriel would do likewise. A thunderclap above the roof would propel the cork from the bottle. Fiery claret would foam. Man and woman would kneel and face each other on the brass bed in a corner of the hut. They would pour the bottle's contents over themselves. Gabriel would lay her down, pull her legs over his shoulders, gaze down on wine-soaked nether lips, and bestow a long Bohemian kiss on the human ferment within.

The wind battering the walls of the hut would be repulsed over and over again, regiments of suicidal rain would be thrown back. How could the bed not become agitated, releasing sparrows and finches from its mattress? How could there fail to be a voice intoning: *may the sheep watch over you?* Finding a shepherd's crook in his hand, Gabriel would lift it high. Woolly ghosts flocking from every corner of the hills would pour into the hut. There would be a miasma, a stench. Infernal bleating would disperse into the night sky and become a galaxy of new stars, spelling plaintive aphorisms for posterity.

The trousers had come to a dead stop. Their owner was speaking into a mobile phone. Gabriel knew that language – a language like an invitation to dine with a professor whose incomparably beautiful daughter you will never meet. It was the language he had been using for thirty years – a language begun in convenience, now overlaid with a detritus of assignations, accusations, tribunals, declarations, and post-its. How had he, the selected one, contrived to follow precisely these trousers?

As he skipped sideways to avoid a collision, he glimpsed a face: long asymmetries of crooked nose, neat teeth, untidy hair, anxious expression prepared for an encounter that would not, could not ever happen, slanted mouth pronouncing clear syllables:

Ja. Ich werde in fünf Minuten bei Marks and Spencers sein.

Gabriel held to his new course and proceeded along Monmouth Street for a considerable while before daring to look back. The trousers had vanished.

TEAR THIS UP

I'm talking about this page
on which the living writer's word is forged
into the likeness of a search
to capture time and render it unstained.

The page describes an ancient villa
where a great aristocrat lies long embalmed
in a bricked-up room at its centre.
No one may approach the tomb.

Climb the sweeping stairs of stone –
on each landing a leaning clock, the torso
of a general, cabinets of clouded glass,
book-pagodas, squealing rats.

Three floors up the ballroom's
parquet glints with shards
of fallen chandeliers. A watchful cat
follows the tread of your shoe.

Light thrusts at dusty windows.
Now the magnet pull of chance reveals to you,
bending down to scoop the cat,
a bare-skinned girl in a ragged gown.

Her gypsy family encamped in far-off salons
are calling out what has to be
her name. She smiles, this chance-
attracting one, at your intrusion.

And you who forge this meeting
return her gaze. How many times must you
return it full to charge the iron of your vocabulary?
All drafts must be destroyed that fail

to place you in the compass of that stare
where whirling sunshaft columns stream
to smash their glittering débris
across a dance floor waiting for its waltz.

BY THE SHORE

i.m Ken Smith

The boat sets out across the water for the island.
I drink a little wine and watch it depart.
The mountains beyond the lake beckon me to climb them.
Too much thinking has made me lazy and fat.

The peat-coloured water cuts open and heals.
I flick through the poems of my friend, then lay them aside.
His charged verses lie speechless in the sunlight.
How faded we all seem now; how we were swept with fire!

The silvery vessel dwindles to a pin-point speck.
The soft-hued sky conjures a dangerous cloud.
I anchor his pages with a coppery ashtray.
The wine glass beside me empties and refills.

Empty tables are scattered under tall trees.
I hold a conversation with his imagined voice.
They've promised us rain; a big drop splashes my forehead.
His answers make me laugh, so funny, so sad.

SUSPECT

The Angel of Death alighted near Holborn Tube.
She wandered down a street and found a park,
a bench, a tree. Colonies of light arrayed the
darkened island. She noticed frowns and soldiers
and papers blowing in an April wind and bags
of things that no one ever counted, not to mention
high-up windows and pale faces looking down
and buses anchored by their scarlet posts and
buildings opening to release the hordes. Before
her stood a single dog. It growled. The Angel
left her bench and walked toward the North.
She heard the gasps and groans and tenderly
collected them and put them in her apron pocket.
She was changing and she knew it. The sun
was frying in the sky. Green leaves were drinking
in the warmth. Not far off the Great Building of
the North would raise its spires and turrets to
the clouds – but how far was it really? Hard to say,
and she was tired. At a brightly-coloured playground
she stopped and entered, talking to the children.
Police arrested her before she did more harm.

THE SOUVENIR

Flames come out of rock and also steam
where the volcano broods and the crater's pit
is silent and the fire spirit needs
a temple, but there is no temple
only wind and sulphur smells…

Those women in the water
stay so long because it flowers warm
from bubbling depths.
I hail them with a wave
and walk the sea-parade of tourist shops.
A lion in a window with
a serpent for a tail
attracts my eye.
It has a vicious goat uprearing from its back.
Too pricey but I buy it.

When we meet she shakes her head and laughs.
Our boat sets out for Kos.
I have a monster in my rucksack,
the sun is warm on chest and shoulders.
For a while I'm absent.

She comes to stand beside me at the rail,
head thrown back, imbibing diesel fumes and
wafts of salt and rosemary.
The question in my head is Seferis:
What is it our souls seek for, travelling
on the decks of decayed ships…?

We cruise the empty workings of the pumice island:
a single jetty, derrick and an empty truck.
Looking at its several peaks
I spot a demon bounding lump to lump
spitting flame from every maw
along the island's broken spine.

My love's blue eyes are catching sun-glints:
"You're brooding aren't you, I can tell."
"I thought I caught a whiff of incense? Or is that smoke."
  She sniffs and looks at me and gestures: 'hopeless',
  rejoins her book and seat.
  I watch her go.

There's a fellow tourist further down the rail.
  His wife is scared of voyages; he's come alone.
  I point to spurts of flame and smoke from the highest points
  on dwindling Nissyros. "You could put a temple there," I say,
"worship at the altar of the Fire Spirit."
  He laughs, and moves away.
The taste of rust and salt is in my mouth
  and silence fills my thoughts –
  the footprints of a gull on air…

We've crossed our stretch of sea.
  I dig into my pack, find the chimaera
  and heft it in my palm.
  No prey had ever dodged it.
  I scan the quay where people smile and wave
  and move toward the other side.
The oily water round our boat plops once.
With that look again, she takes my hand.
The anchor rattles; there's a bump.
We stand with others at the top of iron stairs
  waiting to go down.

STAND UP

You can call it comic or you can call it trouble
but whenever I take my letters to the postbox
I notice once again I've mis-spelt his name –
Schimmelpfennig. Such a bore! He's my doctor
and despite his name he's wagon-loads of fun
except when he gets preacherly about death.

What's the point of going on about death?
It's coming for you and me sure as trouble
and brooding on it takes away the fun
I'm having with the six foot long oak box
I've bought on credit from the Funeral Doctor
where they let you paint it, give the thing a name.

Majestic Slipway Dreadnought is the name
I've given mine. That gets the gravitas into death;
worth doffing your hat to. I'll paint my doctor
on the prow and on the stern I'll write *Trouble
Is My Business* so the worms reading the box
will know to get their friends to join the fun.

I expect you've heard of John Donne? No fun
became the motto of his life. He lived up to his name
and spent his latter days lying in a satin box
practising for the moment of his own death.
Done for! he thought. He saved himself the trouble
of getting well before he died by not calling the doctor.

In those days it was no good getting the doctor.
Medicine was bad soup. A quack's idea of fun
was bleeding you with leeches. He'd look troubled
and say your disease had an unpronounceable name.
Then the angels would sing on the way to your death
and the medics'd write their diagnosis on your box.

Thanks a million, you might have said. But in the box
there's no more talking. No *craic*. Not even with the doctor.
Meanwhile I invent wisecracks on the subject of death
and send them to Schimmelpfennig. It's serious fun.
We're the new comedy team. Soon you'll see our name
at the Trocadero: Sid Shimmy and Todd Trouble.

We'll wear T-shirts sporting *Death Can Be Fun*
and tap dance on a long box. They'll have to call a doctor.
I promise you, we'll give trouble a bad name.

YAGGLE

Yaggle was the word I woke up with.
It was the first thing I said.
What? she said. I said yaggle I said.
Oh no she said and went back to sleep.

I looked out of the window.
Thick grey snow and a thin grey sky.
I hoped the squirrels were in deep coma
in their nest in the linden tree.

What was that you said? she asked
coming into the kitchen. Yaggle I said,
d'you want eggs or muesli?
Her expression said neither.

A crash from below told me
someone was dropping last night's empties
into the bin. She looked at me.
Yaggle down there I said.

I'd put Mingus on the player –
the Stuttgart concert 1964. Eric Dolphy
was scraping phantoms from the walls
and trying out his voice in caves

that were huge and dark and full
of animals. She turned the volume down.
A ton of snow slithered off the roof with a soft *whump!*
Maybe, I said, it will have buried

Herr Snitzschkopf. That would be good.
The toast, she said, it's smoking.
I laid two corpses on her plate.
We didn't speak for a while.

I peeled and ate a tangerine.
Then I peeled and ate another.
I wondered if things were yaggle
with her. Or maybe not yaggle at all.

This is a travesty of a breakfast, she said.
I poured a cup of tea. Nicely brewed I said
want some? Very quietly she
said yes please.

Have I mentioned to you
how beautiful she looks on a Sunday morning
when she has slept well and doesn't
have to go to work?

Going to work – well, it's yaggle.
The Sunday newspapers will discover it soon.
Everywhere people are
thinking about it. Look

at the anxious expressions
of the people in the supermarket queue. It's
yaggle, that's what it is. Pure
yaggle. Try saying it backward

while skipping rope
and catching plastic rings with your teeth
tossed down to you by a seal
on a high pedestal –

that's yaggle for you.
Oh for heaven's sake she said,
the Bloombutters are expecting us at two.
Ah the Bloombutters I said.

Icicles were hanging off the gutters.
When I say icicles I mean heavy torpedos of frozen death.
Imagine I said you're walking along and it's thaw
and one of those things drops off and impales you.

She stared at me.
Life is dangerous I said.
She began to peel an apple,
round and round went the knife

making beautiful circles of skin.
You could try saying it I said. You could utter
everything and nothing all at once. Think how that would feel!
She took a huge bite of the apple and began to chew it.

Yoggle she said.

STILL GRIEVING

On the flyblown mattress of the afternoon
everything's the same and nothing is.
January, I think, come down off your cross;
this clammy August is a fake.

The proper nouns, those dark propensities,
keep hooking gobbets of the real. I'm older by
two minutes. Now sunlight wanders in like Groucho Marx
and sits astride a stool with eyebrows raised.

How did he get here? Time to probe the stairwell's
winding thesis and antithesis. Time to stroll the banks
of the undraggable lake, holding my pale girlfriend's hand.
It's been the wettest summer ever.

On the banks, the fishermen prop rods. Do fish
pay any mind to rain? They're switching on the lights
in cafés. Teeth clink on stealth-lifted teacups. *Sunday
is a wreck!* I want to shout. *It's going down in flames!*

Across the bay of teapots, the moon is rising.
Return from the dead, and I will too. Let's talk about
those awful people with the thick cigars. Let's discuss
if it were ever true my jokes were rude.

I need a medium to help me snag your line… There's
ectoplasm everywhere and garlanded in bladderwrack
I peddle shoddy through the lobby of the Hotel Neptune:
Spectral octopus! Get your spectral octopus here!

Tell me. The time before I was born.
What did you do without me? Who was that fellow on skis?
That smile in the photograph: it's devastating.
What were you trying to say, that last time?